In Search Of Me

Ash'La Johnson
Betty Hawkins

In Search of Me Copyright © 2018 by Ash'La Johnson & Betty Hawkins

All rights reserved. Printed in the United States of America. No part of this book may be used or reproduced in any manner whatsoever without written permission except in the case of brief quotations em- bodied in critical articles or reviews.

ISBN: 978-1-948829-10-6

First Edition: August 2018

Published by
Greater Working Women Publishing, LLC
www.gwwpublishing.com

10 9 8 7 6 5 4 3 2 1

Tired of struggling? Want to know how to overcome them!! You are not alone!!

This is a book of short stories and motivational poems that will assist in your life struggles. This book of life experiences and life lessons will help those that need encouragement, inspiration, and motivation. These poems tells about life challenges and how you can BECOME A SURVIVOR.

As you navigate through this book, you will see how the author experienced firsthand, struggles, obstacles and how "She found happiness and her true self in the midst of those obstacles." This author will let you know "You will make mistakes but it's all in how you handle them." If you want to enrich your life, this is the book you need to lead you to a more peaceful and vibrant life.

TABLE OF CONTENTS

Foreword 2

Introduction 3

My Inspiration 4

Short Stories

The Hook Up 8

It's a Small World 10

It's Morning 13

Poetry

You Had To Know Her 16

A Friend in Deed 18

The Decision 20

Memory 22

New Beginnings 24

Got Away……………………………………………. 26

The Lesson……………………………………….. 28

Thank You…………………………...………….. 31

FOREWORD

There's so many things I want to say, yet not knowing how to begin. It has really been an exhausting, but also emotional journey. I'm writing out of joy, yet experiencing the pain of missing the sound of your voice. You were so full of laughter, a woman with a big heart. Oh did I mention a tad bossy too.

I reminiscence about the mother/daughter discussions we've had together. It was always funny how you would ask me my opinion about a decision you were about to make, then you would turn around and do the opposite. It's one of the things that made you unique. I raised you to make your own choices. In making choices, if you make a bad choice you had to suffer the consequences, but learn from it.

It is my prayer that someone's heart is touched and lives are transformed through the reading of this book of short stories and poetry. I'm glad I got the chance to converse with you on the writing of this project. It never entered my mind that you wouldn't be here to complete what was started. Most of all I'm extremely happy that God allowed me the opportunity to be your mother. I will forever love and miss you, Ashley Dangerfield Johnson aka Ash'La

Your Mom,

Betty McCoy Hawkins

INTRODUCTION

Hello, this is a dream I've had since my adolescent years. I use to write things down whenever anything came to mind. I kept a little notebook that I would write in daily or sometimes weekly. As time passed and I got older, I became interested in other things so I put my notepad away. I threw some things away. I will never make that mistake again, besides it's a great stress reliever.

If you have a dream, no matter how long it takes, pursue it. You should never let anyone or anything deter you from your dreams or purpose. Don't let yourself down. "I can do all things through Christ which strengthens me" (Philippians 4:13). I hope you enjoy!

Ash'La

IN SEARCH OF ME

My Inspiration

Patient, caring, and loving are just a few words that begin to describe the person that has influenced me so drastically in life. She is not only pleasant in spirit, she is also beautiful in sight. The bronze color of her skin resembles a priceless statue on display in one of the world's most prominent museums. Her average yet perfect frame doesn't seem to compare to her year of birth. Although her appearance assures me that when I am her age I will also still be quite attractive. Extending from her light colored scalp are dark-brownish strands accentuated with gray hairs of never-ending wisdom. When she walks in a crowded room her grace and poise is sure to grasp everyone's attention. Although short in statue and shy at times, my role model possesses the biggest heart.

Coming up as a child I watched her give the clothes off her back and food on her plate to those in need. She has housed underprivileged children and treated them as her own, as well as help the homeless. She rarely complains about anything. There have been times I would hear her say "the time you spend bickering about it you could be figuring out how to change your situation". I never understood what she meant until I was able to mature in life. She made sure that every young impressionable person that crossed her path learned something from her that would help them to grow.

As I grew older, the woman who has a great influence over my life became ill. Although going through sickness and her health failing; she never murmured or became bitter. She never ceased her ministry of working with the youth of the church because children were her passion. She often reminded us that her trials are just a test of her faith. She also has a great sense of humor. She loves to laugh and have fun. She has taught me that laughter is good for the soul and smiling is good for the heart. This great woman not only taught me how to be a woman, but she also made sure I learned to be a good wife. I had a great example to live by watching her be a devoted and loving mate to her husband. She made sure I knew how to cook and clean. She would say, "I do not know any man that wants a lazy woman". I blew it off as a child thinking I had plenty of time to learn about being a wife, but being an adult now I respect her for the teachings. She made sure I was brought up in the church and that I respected and treated others as I wanted to be treated. Even to this day she is all about principles and morality.

There have been times I would sit and think to

myself, what a beautiful spirit this creature beholds. She does things out of the kindness of her heart and never reach her hand out for accolades. She is the type of person that loves in spite of mistreatment and gives a smile although she is hurting on the inside. She is not a perfect person and she has flaws but once you meet her you cannot help but love her. Through the years, this influential woman has been my inspiration and my role model. Although she does not own any degrees or awards; it is the loving spirit and divine character that I admire the most in my mother.

SHORT STORIES

IN SEARCH OF ME

The Hook Up

Every day I made it my effort to sit in my office with the door open. I enjoyed watching the handsome, energetic man pass by my door. He passed me daily glancing in my direction, his lips separated only to show his beautiful white teeth. I made sure I smiled back. He seemed like a well-kept individual, always dressed casual. His eyes gave off a glow that showed he was confident with himself. Although we never shared words, his eyes reassured me that he wanted me too.

I watched as he passed by my office briefly from week to week. In the few hours, I was given the pleasure of his presence, I dreamt of his unknown personality. I imagined if his hands and skin felt exactly the way they looked. His skin gave off a radiant look, free of blemish and wrinkle. I yearned to one day be told the history of his hands because they told a story. His hands full of wear and tear appeared scarred. His head shiny and bald was appealing in sight. He was a bow-legged man. Yes, he was quite pleasing to my eyes.

I finally knew what people meant when they

spoke about "love at first sight". I was taught a woman should never approach a man, but yet a man should find the woman. I thought to myself, "If I do not make a move now, I could never get a chance." I knew I had to find the courage to approach him. I stood from my chair, took a deep breath, swallowed my fear and exited my office.

IN SEARCH OF ME

It's a Small World

The year was two thousand seven. My sister and I had just relocated to a new apartment. Once settled in the new apartment, we were satisfied with our new location near a college campus. As time went by, we noticed there were some new neighbors that moved in right below our apartment. Our new neighbors were two African-American gentlemen. They looked as if could have been twins, so my sister assumed they were brothers. As we entered and exited our home daily, we passed our new neighbors without speaking to them. Occasionally, we would wave or just give a smile as a salutation. We never exchanged words or got to know the neighbors. We just went about our everyday lives.

One day, I came home from work exhausted. I twisted the doorknob only to find the door was already unlocked. I was terrified! I thought someone was in our apartment to harm or rob us. I quickly ran down the stairs to the new neighbor's door. I was praying and hoping one of the gentlemen were home. I knocked on the door about three times and what appeared to be the younger of the two came to the door. I explained the situation to him and he volunteered to check the apartment for me before I entered. I thought to myself, "What a really nice guy!" After he checked my apartment I thanked him over and over. He headed back to his apartment and I still never asked his name. Several months had passed; my sister and I decided to move out of the apartment. Though I never got the neighbor's name, I figured I would probably never see him again.

Two years later my sister and I were sitting at my grandmother's house and my cousin walked in with her new boyfriend, Neal. My sister looked at me and we both laughed. Neal was one of our old neighbors, but he was the gentleman that came to my rescue. My cousin and her new beau continued to date for several years. Unfortunately, I still never crossed paths with the other guy from the apartment. I did not want to appear too eager and ask about him.

My cousin and Neal dated for a while and got married in the year twenty-eleven. On the day of the wedding, I walked into the church and saw the other neighbor. After asking a few people about the young man, I found out he was Neal's brother. I was told

IN SEARCH OF ME

that his name was James. Although I was anxious to get to know him, I did not approach him during the wedding. After all the festivities were over everyone went back to their lives and James vanished once again.

My aunt hosted a party in twenty-thirteen and James attended. I was so excited to see him again. He finally decided to approach me and I was nervous. He even brought up the old memories of the day he searched our apartment for me. Our conversation was hilarious. After the party was over, we decided to exchange numbers to keep in touch. We became really good friends as time passed. On weekends we often took walks in the park or went to see a movie. We also traveled occasionally as our time together was priceless. We dated for a while found out that we were quite compatible. After dating for a period of time James proposed marriage to me. James and I enjoyed every minute we spent together. On November seventh of twenty-fourteen James and I became husband and wife.

It's Morning

As the vibration and buzzing constantly rang throughout the two bedroom apartment, James sat with his eyes closed dreading the activities that he knew were going to eventually take place. Even though it was the same repetitive tasks he had to do daily, he still couldn't find the strength to get his eyelids to blossom. As seconds turn into minutes, numerous opportunities came and gradually went by without James giving any progress towards placing his narrow feet on the soft, delicate rug adjacent to his king size sack. As the vibrations continued, James' low protruding exhausted eyes finally begin to blossom and his feet took off across the floor. The room stood gloomy and dark in appearance as if the weather outside was cloudy and the moon was hiding behind the clouds. As he eventually made his way around the room James stopped the vibration and buzzing that began his day.

    Although James was dreading his next step he knew it was all part of the process. He slowly flicked the light switch in the next room adjoining to his bedroom and proceeded to let the cold stream of water fall from the nozzle. James took the cloth laying out from the night before, wet it and rubbed it

IN SEARCH OF ME

across his face. Now aggravated because his eyes were fully opened, James knew a clean mouth was his next assignment. After finishing, he turned and extended his arm behind the blue and gold curtain recently purchased and adjusted the warm flow of water. James was certain this activity would surely do the job of his attempt to have a productive start.

As time flew by, James heard a rumbling and growling coming from his exact location. Then he reflected back on the night before and remembered he didn't have an appetite before bed. Already pressing for time, James knew he must continue his daily tasks without any distractions. James knew that an hindrance would set him an hour behind as it had done a couple days prior. As James completed his final steps and slipped his size ten in his dress shoes, he made his way to the room that never disappoints him. He reached and opened the gray stainless door, James knew something from the box would soon put his rumbling to a halt. With his first meal of the day in his hand, James made his way to the door.

As he turned the knob, James stopped instantly in his path due to an aggressive, unhappy voice flowing from the next room. It was at that moment James wondered what could have been the problem.

James retraced all of his steps and realized he was missing a valuable article from his attire. James proceeded to lean his head in the tall doorway of the adjacent room knowing what was about to transpire. As he looked in the individual's dark, angry eyes his attention shifted to the object swaying back and forth in front of his face. He was ashamed. With his cheeks blushing and full of guilt, he slowly walked across the room and grabbed the object. Holding it with his right hand, James swiftly slid it onto his finger on his left hand. James looked down at his wrist staring at the silver antique birthday gift given to him from the previous year. He immediately realized that he'd wasted too much time. He thought about the long commute to his destination so he released a kiss, shared a moment of embracement and hurried out the door.

POETRY

You Had to Know Her

You had to know her

To understand her

You had to know her

To appreciate the humor

You had to know her

To understand her pain

You had to know her

To see how much in life she'd gain

You had to know her

She had a heart so large

You had to know her

She had to be the one in charge

You had to know her

With her round shapely face

Sitting most of the day

At my mom's house

In her one special place.

You had to know her To understand her dreams

As she made a long deep sigh,

IN SEARCH OF ME

She was just blowing off steam.

You had to know her

My heart sometimes filled with pain

Her angel wings she gained

I'll forever miss her smile

Even the times when she was quite loud.

You had to know her

To understand why.

I will miss her so,

Heaven was waiting

She had to go.

A Friend Indeed

I met a man quite long ago

He gave me love

He gave me hope

I left the man because I was scared

I know I hurt him

I know he cared

I ended up on a road of shame

A road of lust

A road of pain

As time passed I missed the man

Could I return?

Would he withstand?

Withstand my ignorance

And how he was burned

Oh how I missed him

For him I yearned

IN SEARCH OF ME

I dropped to my knees

For his forgiveness I begged

I couldn't make it without this man

He said to me, "No need to fret for

You left me but I never left"

It was at that very moment

I knew this friendship could never end

Because my loving Savior is that kind of friend

The Decision

As she sat amongst the crowd

She knew the end was near

For she wasn't learning nor was she of cheer

She didn't understand how this could be

How he didn't care about losing His sheep

For this was the last time she would sit on that pew

Be a number in the crowd, the others felt it too

They were content but she was afraid

Afraid of the hour of judgement day

She grabbed her purse and ran for the door

This was the Sunday, she couldn't take any more

She never looked back, she wasn't even sad

She was determined to make it to heaven so bad

She drove her car until she came to a stop

She knew she was led there, she knew it was God

He knew she could grow there

IN SEARCH OF ME

He knew she would last

God knew she was ready to take on a task

To regain his love back and live for him

Of course she'd have trials, and plenty of test

Because she was no better than the rest

So just like Job she knew she'd endure

How could she not, she knew God's love is pure

With a forgiving God, a God that doesn't fail

Why would you want to end up in hell

A Memory

I love, I cared

I tried, I shared

I cried so many nights

I know I shouldn't,

It wasn't right but

I thought it was ok

Of course I'm smiling, I'm not sad

Cause that was yesterday

Some days, so weak

Some days, so tired

Some days didn't feel like me

Some days I cried

Some days I screamed, please just let me be

Some days I'm stressed

Some days I strained but

IN SEARCH OF ME

I thought it was ok

Of course I'm smiling, I'm not sad

Cause that was yesterday

Today I'm loved

Today I'm saved

I know I'll be ok

Of course I'm smiling. I'm not sad

I'm living for today

New Beginnings

He loves me, He love me not

At least that what he shown

He tried to play hard to get

So I just moved on

I moved on, but not quite

I tried to leave, without a fight

He knew he messed up

He knew he cared

I ignored his texts, ignored his calls

Didn't want to see, his face at all

I despised him, for leading me on

Even heard rumors, he went back home

Home to the one who broke his heart

Now here I was broken apart.

IN SEARCH OF ME

He shattered my soul and killed all hope

Now I'm filled with darkness, I can't cope

I thought about drinking but that wouldn't help

I thought about dying but he wouldn't care

I thought about smoking but I'd be ashamed

I knew I could pray so I mentioned God's name

My God answered just in time

He gave me a word

He changed my mind

He told me to wait and study his book

He stated his word, "He'll find me and I shouldn't look"

What God has for me shall come to pass

If he said it he meant it

Goodbye to my past

Got Away

I thought we'd be forever

I thought we would last

I believed you were my future

Turns out you were my past

I loved you beyond measure

I took in your pain

I stood by your side

Thru all your rain

I always knew you loved me

You were just too scared to show

By the time you decided to inform me

I was already out the door

I thought you'd one day wake up

And realize what you'd let go

IN SEARCH OF ME

But too much time had passed

And you were a no show

I couldn't wait forever

I knew I must move on

I tried to make you see

I was a woman, I had grown

It's been many years

We know the love's still there

But you took my love for granted

Knowing we were a great pair

I couldn't make you trust me

I couldn't make you stay

Now you regret and realize

I was the one who got away

The Lesson

Life was great, things were good

Until she moved away for school

She met this guy, with such charm

She should've known something was wrong

She thought she could trust him

She thought he was a friend

But that day he took her for a ride

Who'd knew her life would end

No he didn't kill her, well he might as well

It was that night she thought in life she had failed

She thought God had left her

Where could he have gone

She prayed and asked

How could God leave me all alone

IN SEARCH OF ME

She wanted to drop out of school

She couldn't focus in class

Because the night he raped her

Played over and over in her head

She carried her pain for ten hard years

Although she couldn't figure out why

Should be impossible to shed all those tears

With no one seeing you cry

She finally decided to tell someone

And the friend let her know

As long as you keep it in, you'll never let it go

Her rapist had a hold on her

Because she wouldn't move on

She knew if she could overcome this

God would give her a new song

No this isn't for pity and it's not for you to be sad

It is only to help someone

That may have had the same past

It's not what you've been through

It's a blessing you are alive

Now go tell your story on how you survived

IN SEARCH OF ME

THANK YOU

I would like to thank each and every individual for your love and support. You did not have to take the time and show interest in my vision and for that I am sincerely grateful. This is dedicated to the late Mrs. Viola Turner. She inspired me to use the name, Ash'La. That's the name she called me since birth because she couldn't pronounce my real name. A special thanks to my mother, Betty Hawkins, for the encouragement and the idea. This is just the beginning of a journey I have put my faith in pursuing. Again thank you for your support. It is not going unnoticed.

God Bless You All.

With Love,
Ashley Johnson
Ash'La

Betty Hawkins is a native of Monroe, Louisiana. She has served as youth advisor to numerous youth and young adults throughout Northeast, La.

In the midst of the death of her daughter, she found comfort in songwriting and in completion of this book her daughter started. She is committed to helping others live in the right now.

www.ingramcontent.com/pod-product-compliance
Lightning Source LLC
Chambersburg PA
CBHW070752050426
42449CB00010B/2434